THE POETRY OF URANIUM

The Poetry of Uranium

Walter the Educator

Silent King Books

SILENT KING BOOKS

SKB

Copyright © 2024 by Walter the Educator

All rights reserved. No part of this book may be reproduced in any manner whatsoever without written permission except in the case of brief quotations embodied in critical articles and reviews.

First Printing, 2024

Disclaimer
This book is a literary work; poems are not about specific persons, locations, situations, and/or circumstances unless mentioned in a historical context. This book is for entertainment and informational purposes only. The author and publisher offer this information without warranties expressed or implied. No matter the grounds, neither the author nor the publisher will be accountable for any losses, injuries, or other damages caused by the reader's use of this book. The use of this book acknowledges an understanding and acceptance of this disclaimer.

"Earning a degree in chemistry changed my life!"
- Walter the Educator

dedicated to all the chemistry lovers, like myself, across the world

URANIUM

In the nucleus of stars, Uranium lies,

URANIUM

A treasure trove of atomic size,

URANIUM

With eighty-eight protons, it does comprise,

URANIUM

A force of nature that mystifies.

URANIUM

From primordial soup, it arose,

URANIUM

In cosmic furnaces, where chaos flows,

URANIUM

Forged in the heart of celestial glows,

URANIUM

An element potent, its power grows.

URANIUM

In Earth's crust, Uranium sleeps,

URANIUM

In hidden veins where darkness creeps,

URANIUM

A silent guardian, it vigilantly keeps,

URANIUM

Its secrets guarded, as the night weeps.

URANIUM

Miners delve into the earth's embrace,

URANIUM

To unearth Uranium's silent grace,

URANIUM

In caverns deep, they trace and trace,

URANIUM

The essence of this element's face.

URANIUM

From ore to metal, it transforms,

URANIUM

In smelters' flames, where passion storms,

URANIUM

Molten rivers, like fiery norms,

URANIUM

Crafting weapons, or peaceful forms.

URANIUM

But beware the power it holds,

URANIUM

Uranium's tale is oft untold,

URANIUM

Its energy, a double-edged fold,

URANIUM

In cautious hands, its secrets enfold.

URANIUM

Nuclear reactors hum with might,

URANIUM

Harnessing Uranium's inner light,

URANIUM

Generating power, day and night,

URANIUM

A beacon of hope, or a fearful sight.

URANIUM

Yet shadows linger in the wake,

URANIUM

Of accidents, disasters, the earth does shake,

URANIUM

Uranium's legacy, a delicate flake,

URANIUM

In the balance of progress, we make or break.

URANIUM

Beyond the realms of earthly bounds,

URANIUM

Uranium's story knows no bounds,

URANIUM

In space, it whispers without sounds,

URANIUM

A cosmic dance, where destiny confounds.

URANIUM

From the birth of stars to the end of time,

URANIUM

Uranium's journey is an intricate rhyme,

URANIUM

A testament to the sublime,

URANIUM

In the tapestry of the universe's prime.

URANIUM

So let us ponder, with awe and grace,

URANIUM

The wonders of Uranium's embrace,

URANIUM

A symbol of power, a symbol of grace,

URANIUM

In the vast cosmos, it finds its place.

URANIUM

ABOUT THE CREATOR

Walter the Educator is one of the pseudonyms for Walter Anderson. Formally educated in Chemistry, Business, and Education, he is an educator, an author, a diverse entrepreneur, and he is the son of a disabled war veteran. "Walter the Educator" shares his time between educating and creating. He holds interests and owns several creative projects that entertain, enlighten, enhance, and educate, hoping to inspire and motivate you.

> Follow, find new works, and stay up to date
> with Walter the Educator™
> at WaltertheEducator.com

www.ingramcontent.com/pod-product-compliance
Lightning Source LLC
LaVergne TN
LVHW012049070526
838201LV00082B/3870